# Everyday Ordinary People

## (Like a movie, play your role)

Shantise Funchest

Order this book online at www.trafford.com
or email orders@trafford.com

Most Trafford titles are also available at major online book retailers.

Print information available on the last page.

ISBN: 978-1-4907-9283- 5 (sc)
ISBN: 978-1-4907-9282-8 (e)

*Trafford rev.  12/28/2018*

www.trafford.com
North America & international
toll-free: 1 888 232 4444 (USA & Canada)
fax: 812 355 4082

# Contents

# All of a sudden

*The* wind blew furiously knocking the leaves off
the tree
I do not understand what's going on, because it's
spring time how could this be

As I sit on my bed and think to myself
What in the climate control is going on out there,
I'm scared to death?

At first, I thought I was dreaming, but I'm wide
awake and the sun is still beaming

The sky turned dark, but the sun was in plain sight
Something like this usually only happens at night

Still trying to figure out what's going on, I was
glued to the bed with a look of stun

No weather warnings, no live updates
Was the world coming to an end?
Would this be my fate?

I hope it's not too late to make peace with everyone,
even the ones that didn't deserve my apology,
But I was always told forgiveness wasn't for them,
and it was for me

# Same Size Wrong shoes

No one was born into perfection, and no it's something that cannot be taught.
You might wear the same size shoe as the next person, but even if you tried them on you wouldn't be able to walk

You can't feel what they're feeling and your eyes can't see what it is that they see

You were never given that life, it just wasn't yours to live, it never was meant to be

Understand that it is easier said from the outside looking in,
Even you have no control over their life, because there is no entrance

What you can do, is hold your negative criticism and wish them the best of luck

You never know what they're going through, until the shoes are yours to wear.
You might end up with not the best of luck

# Eyes Wide Shut

Do you know what it means to be awake?
I'm not talking eyes being opened, but your
mind as well as your mental state

Don't lose focus, focusing on social media
and all the fake news

For your brain is your toolbox, utilize your tools

There's a lot of misinformed individuals, that
think they know everything, because they got
degrees by finishing school

Well some of these know it all's are mentally
enslaved fools.

Every time something tragic happens, it makes it
to Facebook before it makes it to the news

The government covers it up with what we call a
sleep remedy to hide the truth

Population control is the better word to use, don't
let the cover-ups make you look like a fool.

It's all a distraction and it makes some of us look like a fool
Don't be that lost cause because irrelevance has taken mind control over you.

There's a lot of things that short, but nothing beats life
For life is not to be taken for granted
It is to cherish every moment, to embrace the beauty that comes with living

No one's life is perfect, no glass slippers, no magical horses, but it can be as magical if you want it to be

There's a lot of things that may seem unfair, but life is what you make it and if

# Option V's Priority

Waiting to be accepted, or waiting to be neglected, either way you should accept nothing less than to be respected.
Options are like multiple answers on a quiz while priorities are necessities that you cannot overlook

But then you have some individuals who take advantage and victims who accept anything they do

Just to feel important no matter the hell they're being put through

How much more are you willing to be someone's option?

Never let someone treat you how they think you should be treated

Never overlook the mistreatment and brush it off like it isn't there.

# The black man

The black man is known to be strong, he is known to hide his emotions, no matter what he's going through, but it's only human nature that sometimes the black man cries too.
We laugh at any signs of weakness, but yet we fuss and complain and blame them for being mama's boys for showing any type of emotions and all sorts of other names

We mentally abuse them and degrade their character. We've gotten so comfortable that we don't recognize the mistreatment we put them through

But just any other human being out there, sometimes the black man cries too.

While he's out there fighting the world, he has to come home and fight his woman too

We're too busy being selfish, not realizing how much damage we're putting him through

Sometimes you have to be a man's peace, because just like any other human being, a black man does cry too.

# Vision

There's a light at the end of every tunnel, you just have to find your way out.
No matter what life put you through, life is what you make it about,

As wrongfully as it sounds right now, sometimes in order to make it you have to fake it.

Two steps forward might set you two steps back, but it's not the end of the world

# Starting over

*I*'ve never thought I'd get over you, but I moved on quite well
Never thought I'll open my heart again and rather my life be a living hell

What don't kill you will only make you stronger and it definitely has helped me, prepare myself for my future husband to be

I had to learn to listen, instead of not listening at all
Learn to be considerate and drop those selfish ways

Learn to open up and get pass the break-up stage

# Shattered

*The behavior you've seen displayed earlier comes from an impatient woman
A woman who's had her heart broken many of times*

*A woman who has cried day in and night out*

*A woman who was promised and promise was broken*

*A woman who was once loyal, faithful and trustworthy, so if she gives you a minute of her time you've won a piece of the token*

*A woman with a vengeance to hurt as many men as she could*

*Heart as cold as below zero degrees*

*Let's not forget we're talking about a woman who has cried repeatedly on her knees*

*A woman who once lost faith in men
With a blockage on her heart, because she refuses to let anyone else in*

*A woman who stopped caring*
*A woman who was willing to lose it all*
*Mentally torn apart, and ready for the downfall*

*That woman was weak*
*Drowning in a pool of her own misery*
*No life jacket, no life guards to save her from what*
*would have been her fate*

*That woman was also a woman who got tired of*
*playing the hand that she was dealt and found a*
*way to escape.*

# *Goddess*

*M*edium brown complexion, beard well-groomed handsome man
Yeah, he definitely caught my attention fucked up my whole attention span

Not to mention he was tall with locs and a casual look to match

Undressing him with my mind, nicely built, I assumed he was packing a six pack

Lips nice and full, teeth as white as codeine

Was this goddess available? Should I shoot my shot? Didn't see him sporting a wedding ring

Hazel brown eyes, dimples on both cheek
I'm usually not the approaching type
But if I want to get to know this brother
I needed to speak

They say a closed mouth doesn't get fed and I was definitely hungry,

starving for his attention

My eyes kept roaming this beautiful creation standing right
before my eyes
I wondered if he was really a goddess or a devil in disguise

Well I won't know until I take a chance

I hope he was out here fishing like me and not some woman's cheating ass man

Reapplying my lip-gloss to my lips
I let my ponytail down and headed in his direction

Excuse me sir, he turned around and I got the best reaction

A beautiful smile on his face he asked was I committed
My answer of course was "no"

Well how about around 7 we catch a show

We exchanged each other's numbers and parted our way

I must say today was a good day!

# The wait

Do men still take women they've freshly met out on dates?
Call them to check-up on them, ask them if they need anything and are, they straight

Do they walk around the passenger side and open up the passenger side door?

Call them an ask if they need any groceries while they out shopping at the grocery store.

Do they call out the blue, not expecting to see you, but let you know they miss you?

Send flowers to your job because they want to show you that they appreciate you, for being a part of their life.

Stay up talking to you about nothing on the phone on late nights.

Would they rather spend time with you, instead of spending time with the guys?

*Do they come loyal, honest, faithful and trustworthy too, and not be out here for everybody and won't have you out here looking like a fool?*

*Well I'm looking for him, you might be looking for him too, but I won't be his fool, and it's there's a waiting period for a good man, let me sign up too, and hopefully something will come through.*

# Mirrors

*H*ow dare you shame the woman who's in the picture?
The woman who trusted her heart in the hands of a man

A man that creeps with you, a man that goes home tells her he loves her, while making love to her and at the same time, a man that sleeps with you

How dare you put emphasis on the title that you were given, and step outside your lane

Woman to woman place yourself in that woman's shoes
How come you can't feel that woman's pain?

How come you can't hear her cry? Imagine her burying her face into her pillows at night, when he tells her he's working late, but all the time he's over another woman's house eating off her plate

How dare you mess with a married man, as if there aren't any available men out there who begs for your attention

*How dare you play a dangerous game?*
*With no remorse in your heart*

*How dare you play the victim to circumstance for*
*which you were apart?*

*Did you really think that this man would leave his*
*wife, just to be with you?*

# Brenda

Growing up in a low poverty neighborhood with a dope fiend mother and an absent father
Brenda did all she could
She was just a teenager who was miseducated and mis understood

Some people would always judge her by her parents who were never around
Sometimes it was depressing to go home, so she spent most of her days on the school playground.

She would stay there until the street lights came on
Anything to avoid her mother who was strung out on drugs in some part of their home

Her grades were failing, attendance sort of lacking
With no love at home and suicidal attempts

Brenda stopped second guessing and she began packing

No destination in mind
But what did she have to lose?
She needed to get away from her toxic parents and she was running out of time

As she sat on the living room couch packing the few items that she had,
across from her was her mother laid out on the couch with a needle in her hand.

Tears rolled down Brenda's cheek as she was reminded of the many days the fridge was empty and there was nothing to eat.

The school lunch was always a guaranteed meal, so she ate every opportunity there was, even accepting extras.
Surprisingly no one paid enough attention to question her.

She did have one true friend, who would look out for her from time to time. Sneak her food and clothes, because that's what friends do and she didn't mind.

All the other children parents would come up to the school for assembles, plays and even report card pick-up, but not brenda's parents.
They never showed up, not even one time.

Wishing she had siblings, she was the only child.
Guess there wasn't room for one more

All packed up, with her mother still asleep on the couch, no money for the bus so she began to search the house

After searching every aspect of the house with not a dollar in sight.
Brenda returned to the couch and she began to sigh.

She starred across the room to her mother who was
unconsciously high
and just shook her head and mumbled the words
"why"

She got up quietly and searched the surround
areas, she came across a pocketbook,
with a fifty-dollar bill inside it and that's what she
took.

She grabbed her duffle bag and jacket and headed
out the door.
She knew it was time for her to be out on her
own and with a plan in mind she vowed to never
return to her mother's home.

But she did wonder if her mother would come
looking for her probably not

She was too busy in her own little world,
with a serious drug addition, that prohibited her
from taking care of her very own baby girl.

Brenda knew no family, other than her parents so
she was all alone
In a cold world she traveled
She didn't know what was worse,
Living out on the streets or being a victim in her
mother's home

She got tired of suffering, watching her mother kill
herself slowly
With money for her addiction, but Brenda
received hand me downs
from the local church charities and neighbors
knowingly.

First night of being out on her own, she slept in a rundown motel room which she called her home.

She filed out job applications at the local diners and coffee shops
She was determined to make a way for herself
No matter how difficult life became she wasn't going to stop.

The next day one coffee shop hired her at minimum wage working 30 hours a week.
It might not have been much to others, but it was enough for her to get on her feet.

Dedicated to the job that she was blessed to have
With outstanding attendance and customer service skills,
her manager wanted to give her a higher position and pay

Thankful for the opportunity that was stumbled upon
She now could afford a better place to stay.

# Unexpected

*H*e said he never met a girl like me.
*It* was my beauty, my honesty and most of all
my loyalty,

But that wasn't enough to lock him down
He never felt the need to invest in me

Guess I expected too much in return
I felt like if I really wanted to be with this man
I had to wait my turn

But, I've always wondered if he was afraid of
commitment?
Or was I even ready to be committed to?

Why do we chase the ones who don't want us, and
ignore the one who do?
Ignoring their phone calls and text messages
Adding them to the block list too

Sometimes the heart makes unexpected decisions,
before the mind can even make a move.

They say you'll know when a man really wants to
be with you

Well I don't agree with that statement; these men play games too.

I done been in situations where they'll lead you on knowing their minds already been made up
And have you out here looking like a fool

Some may genuinely want to be with you and others just look at you as beneficial

But those are the chances that you take and see where it leads you.

# Grown Woman

Never have I been the type to care what others
think of me
I've always thought highly of myself you see

I work a 9 to 5 and pay my own bills
Get off of work, go home kick my feet up, relax and
chill

Pour a glass of wine, watch a little television
Maybe go to a lounge and mingle a bit
Whatever I choose it's my decision

Remember grown women do what they want
While lil girls do what they can

But one thing I've never done and that was
intentionally sleep with another woman's man

# Blockage

*Silly of me to think that you were different from the rest*
*You continue to prove me wrong, after failing many assessment test*

*I gave you a chance, fell in love with you, even thou I gave up on love a long time ago,*

*I promised myself to never let another man steer me in the wrong direction*

*Instead of wasting my time, I could of easily accepted the rejection*

*You want to be considered a man, but under what grounds?*
*A man that's a real man will prove he's a real man, without making any sound*

*Real men move in silence, guess you never got that memo*
*But I never saw what we had coming to an end thou*

*Am I too much for you? Do I intimidate you?*
*Is a relationship getting in the way?*

*Are you seeing someone else, in love with someone else, and you don't know the proper words to say?*

*So, tell me what's going on, why waste another day?*

# Image V's Character

A reason to be conceited, yet looks slowly deteriorate
Outside of a nice body and a pretty face
What else do you have to secure that man's taste

You're mistaken if you think you can't be replaced
He'll go out there and find a woman with a not so cute face

One who's not easy to replace, but she'll have something going for herself, and bring more to the table

More than what you have to give, because she too will understand that appearance does not define who you are, but it does give you an image, that'll only last for so long

So again, tell me how conceited you really are?
Keep living that fairytale life, that'll only get you so far.

# Yeah, those people

You know those people that have an answer for everything,
Always right, never wrong
Can't tell them nothing, give them your opinion or advice
Toss items in the shopping cart, not worried about the price,

"Yeah, those people"

The ones that think someone owes them something, but haven't earned nothing at all
The one who plans events, yet shows up late,
And play victim to circumstances for which they create

Can't take them nowhere, because they'll embarrass the hell out of you

Complains about their paycheck being short, but calls off all the time
Keeps their money to themselves, while borrowing money from others, with no intentions on paying them back a dime

The ones who'll argue with you about whether the
earth is round or flat
Never want to talk on the phone, always want to text

"Yeah, those people"

The ones who immediately fix plates as soon as
they come to an event
Take mad vacations, but struggling to pay the rent

Complaining about how many kids someone else
got, but won't lift a hand
Always bragging about how they done stole
somebody's else man

Still staying with their mother, but swear they're
helping her out
Sleeping in your aunt's basement, or upstairs on
her couch

We know those who fix extravagant meals, but
kids eating something else
How do you not put your kids before yourself?

Christmas come ridiculous number of gifts beneath
the tree, but yet still no window curtains, and the
only privacy you got are whatever is held up by
the sheets

A dirty kitchen, but yet will still cook a meal
Unemployed, no desire to work, but always want
to chill

Yeah those that I'm referring to,
I know a few of those and I'm sure you do too

# Oh, it's Monday again

Not one, but three times, I've snoozed the alarm, not wanting to get up
I can't believe its Monday all over again, now I'm just lying here, stuck

But someone has to make the money, it won't make itself

I need a guide on how to deal with Mondays, lord knows I need help

I'm always a little late for work, sadly to say,
Did I mention it only happens on Mondays by the way?

Every work hour on Mondays seem to go pretty slow, even when you're not watching the time

Working on a Monday should be considered a crime

But if we get rid of Mondays, Tuesdays would be hated next
Let me stop procrastinating about Mondays and get up and get dressed

# Lonely

*It's never a good feeling when you're in a relationship, but the feeling of loneliness awakes you*
*Your significant other has no idea of all the suffering and stress that they're putting you through*

*Some are selfish, inconsiderate and some without a care, no matter how they treat you, you've shown them that you'll always be there*

*People take your kindness for weakness, so use to everyone else letting them slide*

*Even after they're in the wrong, no apologies, too good for their own pride*

*Apologies only hurt the weak.*
*They become intimidated so to speak*

*They become afraid to face their own kind*
*As if they're in a courtroom facing twelve jurors, as if they're were fighting a murder crime.*

*Immune to the society now days,*

Where women are of lesser value and men have
their way

Nothing to work for, because it's so freely given
Grown women mistaken for little girls, but hey it's
the world we live in.

# Double Standards

You can bring everything to the table,
But will it get that man to eat?

After working double hours on the clock will he massage your feet?

Will he prepare dinner as if the tables were turned?

Will he sit back take notes, eager to learn?

Will he try to understand you and read your mind, be 100% and not waste your time?

Will that man get up and go for it?
Will you keep your standards high or will you lower them?

Will you show him what you want and not what you need?
Show him that without him you'll be independent and not dependent because that's not what you need

# Art of Seduction

*I* want to be able to roll over and tell you good morning, instead of texting
Me on top of you, tongue deep down your throat at the same time while I'm sexing you

Hands wrapped around my waist as you lift me up and down

Juices running down my leg, suppressing moaning sounds

I bend down a little further and let the metal hit your lip

You open wide enough just to get a mouth full, as you continue to massage my insides

Enough of the riding, instantly flip me on my backside

Lift up my legs dive in face first
Twirl your tongue around my pearl tongue and in between my thighs

Send electrical chills down my spine
Legs over my head as you insert, your manhood
inside this place that we call the honey comb
hideout

# Existence

Speak to my heart, massage my
mind with your intelligence

Embrace my heart with your love, and
touch my soul with your uniqueness

# FrOm SiNnErS 2 SaInTs

*Endless nights where I couldn't sleep.*
*Phone constantly going to voicemail, because you rather run the streets*

*Never letting anything get in the way of you taking care of your family*

*Until I got that call that night,*
*I knew deep down in my heart something just wasn't right.*

*Rushing into the emergency room, heart beating off track*
*As I got a step closer to the room*

*The surgeon stopped me in my tracks, and closed the door shut*
*Not knowing what to expect next,*
*I rerouted myself back to the lobby area and re read our text*

*The last text we sent was me telling you to be careful and you replied, "Baby I will"*

But right after that I got that phone call that gave me chills and I asked myself, "Was this some sick joke?" or was this really real"

I didn't care what procedures they had to do,
All I knew is I just couldn't stomach losing you.

# Feelings

*The* objective to the game was to not catch feelings,
As easy as said, but how can you not catch feelings for someone who gives you quality time,

Someone who fulfills that void where the previous person left behind in just a matter of time

The compatibility is what makes us. Consistency is what keeps us at existence,
Not to mention, even thou you got a girl I've always played my position

Never stepped outside of boundaries
Never done anything to jeopardize your relationship, but tell me how could you love someone and not give them your all?

Someone you claim, who have your back and stayed down for you

Why not turn in your player card with the things you put them through?

# King

When a man proves that he's a man of his word,
He too becomes king of his castle and
he leads his queen to greatness

# Heartless

*It* would be nice to hear birds chirping and
children playing outside,
But the only thing you hear are the sounds from
the gunshots and sirens,

Never once have you heard anyone say, "let's come
up with a solution" and actually going along with
the plans to stop this violence

The violence is spread-out all-over Chicago from
the north to the south,

But you all are sleeping with these killers, housing
them, feeding them, taking care of them, but yet
no one wants to open up their mouth

If they can act without a conscious and commit a
senseless crime,
What makes you think you're not the alternative
waiting next in the retaliation line?

If they can't get to you, it's perfectly fine
A life for a life they'll just sits back and steal your
bloodline

It's not so much of it being just a retaliation thing

*The innocent die so young behind the scenes*

*Some of them never got a chance to grow into adults*
*Something must give this city needs help*

*Something must give,*
*So, the younger generation can live*
*We need doctors, lawyers and teacher on site, but we'll be left with nothing, because we keep losing a life*

# Karma

Was it love or was it lust?
Were the feelings mutual or were it just something to do?

Convenience or loneliness, what's easier to get through?

One of us caught feelings that were stronger than the other,
Even after knowing what it was from the start

Spending excessive amount of time with each other,
made it difficult for someone to play their part

Seeing you multiple times a week,
Really has changed my view on the way I see men so to speak

But I spoke too soon, you were just like the rest
Maybe God placed me into your life, so karma can finish the rest

# When a woman's fed up

You say you want a down ass chick,
But yet you still treat her like shit

Beating on her, cheating on her
Passing around community dick

You claim you want a real ass chick, but how real
do you think it gets
You're dealing with a woman who's constantly
putting up with your shit

Do you ever sit back and think about all the
craziness you've put her through?

It's called madly in love, that woman really loves you

When a woman's stays with a man she believes in
him and believe he'll change, but after repeatedly
breaking her heart, things will never be the same

It might take some time to finalized the break-up
When a woman's fed up

But when she's fed up there is no coming back
She'll treat you as if you've never existed and
that's a fact

# The temp

The dust blew him my way.
The broom swept him away.
He did not belong to me; therefore,
he could not stay!

# Loyalty

There's beauty without brains, but what do you prefer?
After while beauty deteriorates, and what are you left with?
A below average chick who once was a bad bitch

Hair stayed done, eyelashes and brows on fleek, but can't bring the dishes to the table and make you all a plate, when it's time for you all to eat

If you fell off right now would she pick up the slack?
Would she have your back, without you having to ask?

Would she change positions and still know her role?
Or would she be your chauffeur driving you down that lonely road?

Would she pick up the tab at the end of the dinner date?
Would she put her wants off to the side, just to make sure that you all are straight?

Would she lift up your spirit during your down time, and assure you that she got this and everything will be alright because she'll always be around?

Would she be your peace without you having to leave and support the goals that you're trying to achieve?

Would she put it all into actions, instead of talking about what all she'll do?

Is she only around for what you can provide? Will she swallow her pride when it's time to switch sides?

Would she keep her honesty and loyalty to you, or would she play you like a fool and mess with other dudes?

Would she be a life jacket and keep you afloat or would she watch you drown by poking holes in your boat?

# Too be scene

He who seeks validation has
insecurities within himself
He must seek counselling, so that
he can get the proper help

# Living your best lie

*How could you be living your best life posting all those social media stats full of drama?*
*Putting your business on Facebook, seeking validation from strangers*

*Talking about how the dude who you had a baby with ain't shit, but yet this the man you let between your legs, you know the one you laid down with*

*How could you be living your best life, but always want to fight?*
*It takes two to tangle, but someone has to be the bigger person and say you know what this isn't even worth it*

*How could you be living your best life, but yet throwing subliminal messages*

*People who are living their best life are also living a personal life*
*There's no need to address it*

# Beneficial

*If* you can't finance her, you don't need to be
fucking her,
simple as that

y'all men got the game confused, and most of y'all
need a reality
check

y'all think y'all can lay up with a woman and not
pay where you lay your head

Don't pull the sheets back unless you're willing to
make up that woman's bed

Unless you're willing to make up that woman's
bed, don't even have a seat

We all hustler's out here, we all trying to eat

What you won't do the next man will
He'll love what you failed to love and while loving
her he'll pay her bills

He'll take care of the minor things you complained
about,

Without a doubt she'll count you out

You'll then try to buy your way back in, but
by that time she done already moved on to
another man.

# Fix your crown

**N**ever ever will I again put my life on hold
Sit back in the cut waiting on things to unfold

I placed my heart in your hand to hold. You have
no conscious of breaking it, "How bold"

Came to you with what's bothering me
You shook me off in a selfish way
Making it difficult to bring anything else your way

Thought we were a team
At least that's the way you made it seem

While I was cheerleading for you,
you were trying out for the next team

I treated you like a king,
and I expected to be treated like a queen.

The queen that I am and will always be
I was two steps forward, while you fell three steps
in back of me

A queen doesn't step off of her thrown to address a
peasant
Karma's a bitch and life's a lesson

# Intimidated

*N*ever believe someone when they say they
need their space
What they really want to tell you, they're too
intimidated to say it to your face

So, they string you along, in hopes you'll
eventually give up and you both will go your
separate ways,

But then you have to find out for yourself what
their intentions really were

# Focus

Have you ever been so focused, that everything
outside of your comfort zone became irrelevant?

*"Negativity could not exist"*

People invite negative energy into their lives
It doesn't just show up and say, "Hey I'm the bad
vibe, how about you open up and let me inside".

Why prove a point,
when you really don't have to?

# Hellbent

The hate be so real and the love be so fake
Couples stay in toxic relationships, just for the benefits
I think I was born in this world a little too late

No one wants to put in the work
People don't fight for love anymore

Walking on a shattered glass floor
It'll save you the headache, by simply walking out the door

Why are we so impatient when it comes to love, what's the urgency?

# Mommy's little girl

When I complain, you say that I'm tripping
Whenever I ask you for something, that's
when you go missing

My mama has always been there, because she
cares
It takes two to make a baby, but you act like you
wasn't there

Never thought the impossible, man this right here
isn't fair
It has always been fuck my feelings, as if you
don't care

But daddy you showed me the real you,
and a deadbeat is exactly what describes you

as much as you weren't around
my mother never talks down on you

she always told me one day I'll see the real you
none of that was a lie, she was telling the truth

# Cheat in peace

*I* can't even cheat in peace,
this man keeps face timing me

I can't even go to sleep,
he's stalking all of my dreams

accusing me of cheating like you have a reason,
Staying late nights on Sunday nights like you been
praising Jesus

but you don't even believe in Jesus, so why do you
have a Jesus piece

if you want out, then leave, but you can't keep
accusing me

portraying your role, like you really have love
for me
when all you care about is other women and that's
obviously

I thought you was a real man, where's your
loyalty?
You're messy, but you want to address me and
stress me

You use to accuse me of cheating all the time, but we both know who were the one who was really lying

Whenever I'm in these streets, you got your people spying
I can only chase money right now, I ain't got no time

You think I'm stupid because I never ever confronted you baby,

You out here living a single life, I'm just being honest baby

You don't even reply to my text quick, but you have no problem passing out community dick

I got different men waiting in line, begging me for my time

Ain't no loyalty, you lied to me
All you do is run the streets

# Dedication

There's no fragrance that's more refreshing,
than the fresh smell of cleaning products while
cleaning your home
Powder fresh linen, white walls
Waxed floors and sparkling marble counter tops

Those are the side effects, that comes along with a
clean house

Smudge free mirrors, vacuumed rugs and crystal-
clear table glass top

Self-cleaned oven, clean toilet bowl
Tossing everything out of the fridge that's old

Dishes inside the dish washer on an hour wash
I know some who are neat freaks and some who
are just lost

I'll have a glass of wine while dinners on the stove,
A basket full of clothes which I have to fold

Once dinners all done, make the kids plate
Bathe them, tuck them in bed
There's no staying up late

*Wait on the Mr. to come in from work*
*Plate fixed and clothes laid out*

*That's the married life most of y'all don't know about*

# Pass the past

*The mind wonders, the heart bleeds profusely
The eyes are intense as the sorrow covers the oxygen supply*

*Dark clouds take over the beautiful sky, leaving behind a thousand why's*

*The lump in your throat freezes, preventing you from expressing yourself*

*The tears create a blockage to your peripheral vision, making it hard to see pass the past*

*Alone is what you've become, trapped in your own sorrow*

*You've become that person, who lives in the past, Afraid to strive for future change*

*Anything that would make life greater
Anything outside of remaining the same*

# Adulthood

We rush to be adults, but then when we get to that stage,
We wish we could go back in age

Our parents made it look easy, and they did one hell of a job
Never wanted for anything and was always fed
Clean clothes and a shelter over our heads

Never known for any bills to be past the due date
I'm almost certain they were, because I don't always pay on time, they'll get their money late

Paying bills and stretching money to make things work out
Now I know what my parents were talking about and this adult shit isn't working out

# The land of the free

Seeing whoever I want
Interacting with whoever I want
Never putting my all into just one
person, to waste my time
Going out with whomever I like
Living my single life as I like
Entertaining whoever I like

Printed in the United States
By Bookmasters